Student Solutions Manual to

Accompany

Health Economics, second edition

Student Solutions Manual to Accompany

Health Economics, second edition

Frank A. Sloan and Chee-Ruey Hsieh

The MIT Press

Cambridge, Massachusetts

London, England

ISBN: 978-0-262-51790-4

10   9   8   7   6   5   4   3   2   1

Contents

Solutions to Odd-Numbered Exercises

Chapter 1

Introduction and Overview

1.1   Suppose the government in a middle-income country announced its policy goal was to implement a universal health insurance program within five years. Would implementation of this policy increase the demand for health economics research in this country? List at least three factors to justify your answer no matter whether your answer is "yes," "no," or "maybe."

The implementation of a universal health insurance (UHI) program is expected to increase the demand for health care and hence to expand the size of the health care sector within a country. As more resources are being allocated to the health sector, it would increase the demand for research to understand many important questions such as whether resources devoted to health care are used efficiently. In addition, the implementation of a UHI program increases demand for understanding potential effects of various health policies such as the payment systems and cost-sharing. This provides an incentive to public agencies to grant research in this area in order to learn the "know-how" of designing an efficient public health insurance program. Furthermore, the implementation of a public health insurance program may generate public use data, which in turn provides material for to conducting research on these topics.

Chapter 2

Health and Health Behaviors

2.1   A patient with arthritis of the knee is planning to have a knee replacement. He has applied for a loan for this surgery; the loan has an annual interest rate of 6 percent. The artificial knee can function for 10 years before it needs to be replaced. Fees for knee replacement surgery are expected to grow at 5 percent annually.

a. Why is an artificial knee a form of health capital?

An artificial knee can serve as a body part for several years, which is similar to capital stock that yields a flow of returns annually.

b. Assume the artificial knee depreciates at a constant rate every year until the time of replacement, which is 10 years hence. What is the cost of this capital?

The cost of capital (COC) = $i + \delta - a$, where i indicates the cost of obtaining a dollar of capital for a period, δ is the depreciation rate on the capital stock, and a is the appreciation rate of a unit capital. In this case, $i = 0.06$, $\delta = 0.1$, $a = 0.05$. Thus, COC = $0.06 + 0.1 - 0.05$ = 0.11.

c. Suppose that instead of a loan, the patient plans to pay for the surgery from his or her own savings. Assume that the bank's interest rate on savings deposits equals its rate on loans. Does this change your answer to (b)? Why or why not?

COC remains the same in this case because the use of personal saving has an "opportunity cost." That is, this patient needs to give up the return from his or her own saving in order to pay the surgical fees. This opportunity cost equals the bank's interest rate on savings deposits.

d. Draw the COC (cost of capital) line on a graph, with health capital on the x-axis and the COC rate on the y-axis. What is the slope of the COC schedule? Explain why it looks the way it does.

The COC line has a zero slope, that is, it is a horizontal line because the individual investment on health does not change the market value of i. Also, δ and a are constants and do not change with the amount of health investment.

2.3   Assume the health production function is $h = 365 - 1/H$, where h is the number of healthy days a person has in each year and H is the person's health capital. Assume this person earns a wage of \$100/day, and the marginal cost of health investment $\pi = 25$ and is constant over time. The annual interest rate is 5 percent, and health capital depreciates at a rate of 15 percent per annum.

a. What does the MEC for this person's health capital look like? Draw the MEC curve on a graph, with health capital on the x-axis and the rate of return on the y-axis. Explain the shape of this MEC curve.

$MEC = (w \cdot G)/\pi$, where w is the wage rate, π is the marginal cost of health investment, and $G = dh/dH = 1/H^2$. Given the values in this question ($w = 100$, $\pi = 25$), $MEC = 4/H^2$. Based on this function, MEC is a downward sloping curve as follows:

MEC (y-axis)	4	1 (4/4)	0.44 (4/9)	0.25 (4/16)
Health (x-axis)	1	2	3	4

b. What is the cost of health capital in this problem?

The cost of capital (COC) = $i + \delta - a$. $i = 0.05$, $\delta = 0.15$ and $a = 0$.
Thus, COC = 0.20.

c. Find the optimal level of health this person demands under the above conditions.

The optimal level of health capital is solved by setting MEC = COC.
That is, $4/H^2 = 0.20$. Thus, $H = \sqrt{20} = 4.47$.

d. Suppose the person acquires a *chronic disease* and his health depreciation rate rises to 35 percent annually. How does this change your answer to part (c)?

COC = 0.05 + 0.35 = 0.40. The optimal level of health capital is solved using $4/H^2 = 0.40$. $H = 3.16$. This is the optimal level of health capital decreases because the user cost of capital increases.

e. Suppose instead of having a chronic disease the person experiences a recession and his wage falls to $50/day. Assume the change in the price of time inputs changes the cost of a unit of health investment by 10 percent. Show graphically how this change affects the MEC curve. What is the person's optimal health demand now?

In this case, w falls to 50 and π falls to 22.5 (see answer 2.3a), then MEC $= 50/(22.5 \cdot H^2) = 2.22/H^2$. The MEC shifts to the left and the optimal level of health capital falls to 3.33, which is obtained from $2.22/H^2 = 0.20$.

f. Now focus on the role of human capital in this model. Suppose a person's educational attainment increases. How does the MEC curve shift in this case? How does this shift affect the person's investment in health capital?

An increase in a person's educational attainment increases efficiency in health production and hence reduces the marginal cost of health investment. The MEC schedule shifts to the right and hence increases the person's optimal health capital stock. However, higher educational attainment is positively associated with wage rates. Higher wage rates make investments in health care more costly. But they also increase the benefit from investment in health since avoiding sick days becomes more valuable. Thus, the effect is ambiguous a priori.

2.5   Suppose a person is asked a standard gamble question about three kinds of diseases. For each disease, the person decides to undergo surgery if the expected utility from the operation exceeds or is equal to the patient's utility if he or she does not undergo surgery and continues having the disease. The person's expected utility is therefore $(1 - \theta)U_a + \theta U_d$, where U_a is the utility if the operation is successful, U_d is the utility if it fails (and the person dies), and θ is the probability of failure. The patient assigns the following probabilities of surgical failure to the diseases:

Disease	A	B	C
θ	0.25	0.4	0.01

a. Assume $U_a = 1$ and $U_d = 0$. Then what is the utility of having each of the diseases if the person is indifferent between having and not having the operation?

The utilities of being in disease states A, B, C are 0.75, 0.6 and 0.99 respectively, which are calculated from $1 - \theta$.

b. If the diseases are liver cancer, pneumonia, and dental caries, which one is most likely to be denoted as A above?

Disease A is likely to be pneumonia, disease B is likely to be liver cancer, and disease C is likely to be dental caries.

Viscusi and Evans (1990) took a similar approach to analyzing the loss in utility from being healthy to becoming sick. In the experiment they discussed in their paper, workers were randomly assigned to label four different chemicals: asbestos, TNT, sodium bicarbonate, and chloroacetophenone. The first two chemicals are quite dangerous and could cause death if they exploded. The third is rather harmless, and the fourth will only cause some tearing if proper treatment is not received. The authors asked the workers how much money they would have to receive in compensation if they were reassigned to label another chemical. We will now apply the standard gamble concept to this problem. Assume the workers' utility function is $U(w) = \ln w$, where w is the hourly wage received from the labeling work and $U(\text{death}) = 0$.

c. The probability of TNT exploding is θ_{TNT}, and if it explodes, the worker cannot survive. Also suppose the wage for labeling sodium bicarbonate is w_S per hour. What is the minimum wage a worker must receive if he were reassigned to label TNT as a function of θ_{TNT} and w_S?

The minimum wage a worker must receive to label TNT (w_{TNT}) must satisfy the following condition:
$\theta_{TNT}U(\text{death}) + (1 - \theta_{TNT})U(w_{TNT}) = U(w_S)$. This equation reduces to $(1 - \theta_{TNT})\ln w_{TNT} = \ln w_S$ by substituting $U(w) = \ln w$ and $U(\text{death}) = 0$ into the equation. Thus, $w_{TNT} = w_S{}^A$ with $A = 1/(1 - \theta_{TNT})$.

d. Which labeling work must have a higher wage, asbestos or chloroacetophenone?

Asbestos.

e. What is the wage function for chloroacetophenone? Use w_S as the benchmark again. Which value(s) do you need to be able to solve this problem?

Following the same approach shown in question c, the wage function for chloroacetophenone $(w_c) = w_s^{B}$ with $B = 1/(1 - \theta_c)$, where θ_c indicates the probability of causing some tearing.

f. One major implication of Viscusi and Evans's research is that people may have different utility functions when healthy than when sick. Suppose the utility function is $V(w) = 0.5\ln w$ if the worker is sick but alive. How does this change your answer to part (e)?

The answer is the same as the answer to part (e).

Chapter 3

Demand for Health Care Services

3.1   Suppose a demand curve has the form $x = 100 - 10p$. What is the quantity consumed at $p = 5$? What is the elasticity of demand at $p = 5$? Suppose the demand curve is a demand curve facing the firm, such as a physician's office. At what level of p is marginal revenue zero? Why may the demand curve for the firm have a negative slope? When marginal revenue is zero, what is the price elasticity at this level of p? Would giving the patient a $5 subsidy per visit tend to increase or decrease the elasticity of demand? Justify your answers.

The quantity consumed at $p = 5$ is 50, which is calculated as $x = 100 - 10 \cdot 5$. The elasticity of demand evaluated at $p = 5$ is: $(dx/dp) \cdot (p/x) = (-10) \cdot (5/50) = -1$. By definition, total revenue (TR) equals the product of price and quantity. $TR = p \cdot x = [(100 - x)/10] \cdot x = 10x - (x^2/10)$. Marginal revenue (MR) $= dTR/dx = 10 - (x/5)$. Set $MR = 0$ to get $10 - (x/5) = 0$. Solve this equation to get $x = 50$. Inserting this value ($x = 50$) into the inverse demand equation, $p = (100 - x)/10$, we obtain $p = 5$. At $p = 5$, $MR = 0$.

The demand curve has a negative slope for two reasons. First, there is a substitution effect: as the price of the physician visit increases, the patient may use other goods (such as over-the-counter drugs) or services (such as self-care) to substitute for physician visits. Second, there is an income effect: as the price of the physician visit increases, the real income (or purchasing power of a given household income) decreases. Thus, the demand for physician visits as well as demand for all other goods or services decreases as long as these goods or services are normal goods.

The subsidy will not change the slope of the demand curve (dx/dp remains unchanged) but will cause the demand curve to make a parallel shift to the right. This implies x increases as p remains constant and hence p/x decreases. This subsidy *decreases* the elasticity of demand in absolute terms. The patient becomes less responsive to a price change in the presence of the subsidy.

3.3   An individual has preferences for an aggregate consumption commodity (*x*) and health (*H*) represented by a utility function $U(x, H) = \alpha\ln(x) + \beta\ln(H)$. The price of the aggregate commodity (*x*) is p_x and the price of medical care (*m*) is p_m. The input of medical care (*m*) produces health (*H*) via a health production relationship that can be represented by the function $g(m) = \ln(m)$; that is, $H = \ln(m)$.

a. Compute the optimal demand for medical care (*m*), the aggregate consumption commodity (*x*) and health (*H*) as functions of prices (p_x, p_m), income (*y*), and the parameters of the model (α, β). You may assume a standard budget constraint.

The optimal demand for medical care is derived by maximizing utility subject to income constraint. Mathematically, we obtain the first-order conditions from the following Lagrange Multiplier equation: $L = U(x, H) + \lambda(y - p_x x - p_m m)$. Using the following functional form, $L = \{\alpha\ln(x) + \beta\ln(\ln(m))\} + \lambda(y - p_x - p_m)$.

First Order Conditions:

$$\partial L/\partial x = 0, \quad \alpha/x = \lambda p_x \tag{1}$$

$$\partial L/\partial m = 0, \quad \beta\,(1/\ln(m))(1/m) = \lambda p_m \tag{2}$$

$$\partial L / \partial \lambda = 0, \; y = p_x \, x + p_m \, m \tag{3}$$

b. Calculate the price elasticity of demand for medical care.

Based on the above result, we calculate the price elasticity of demand for medical care (ε) as follows:

On both sides of (2) take the derivative of m with respect to p_m

$$(1/m)[-\beta/(\ln m)^2 \cdot (1/m) \cdot dm/d\,p_m\,] + (\beta/\ln m) \cdot [-1/(m^2) \cdot dm/d\,p_m] = \lambda$$

Then $(dm/d\,p_m\,)(-\beta/m^2\,)(1 + \ln m)/(\ln m)^2 = \lambda$

$$dm/d\,p_m = (-\lambda\,/\beta) \cdot [(m \ln m)^2/(1 + \ln m)]$$

$$\varepsilon = dm/d\,p_m \cdot (p_m\,/m)$$

$$= (-\lambda\,/\beta) \cdot [(m \ln m)^2/(1 + \ln m)] \cdot (p_m\,/m)$$

$$= (-\lambda\,/\beta) \cdot [(\ln m)^2/(1 + \ln m)] \cdot (p_m \cdot m)$$

3.5 The following questions concern the use of deductibles.

a. Show the effect graphically of a deductible on the demand for medical care.

Assume no insurance coverage initially. Then assume there is an insurance policy with a $500 deductible. The price of medical care is $50 per unit. After the deductible is satisfied, the health insurance plan pays for 75 percent of expenses.

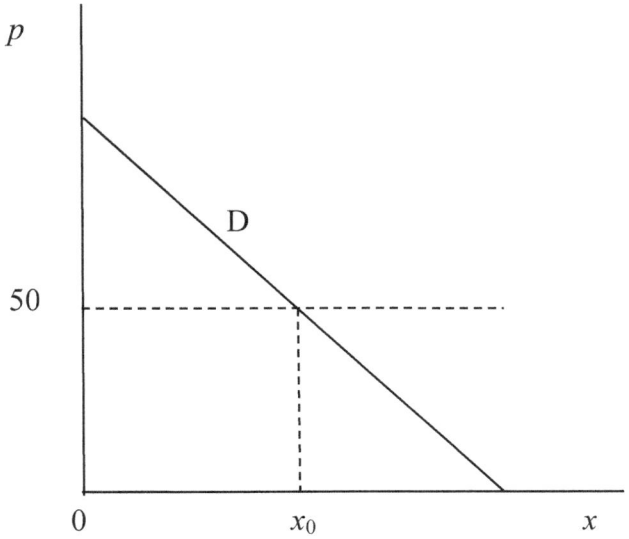

Initial case: no insurance coverage

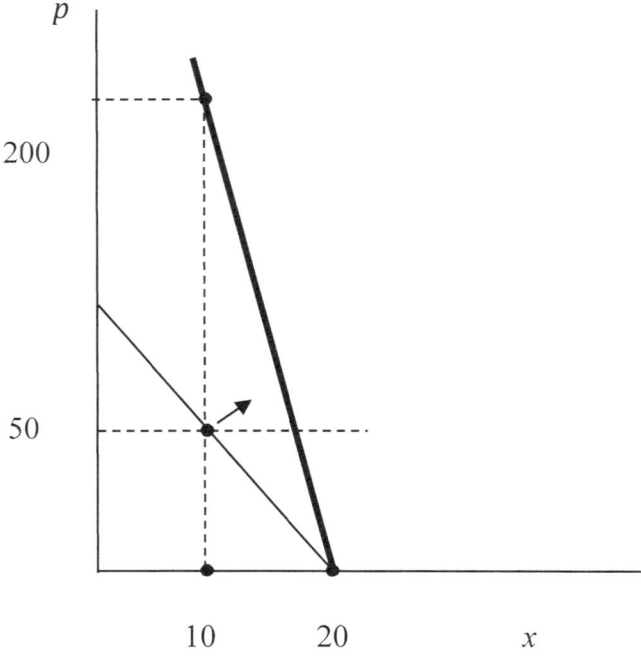

The original demand curve has points (10, 50) and (20, 0) on it. With 25 percent coinsurance, a price of 200 elicits a demand of 10. So the points (10, 200) and (20, 0) are on the new demand curve. Thus, the new demand curve rotates outward and is represented here by a bold line.

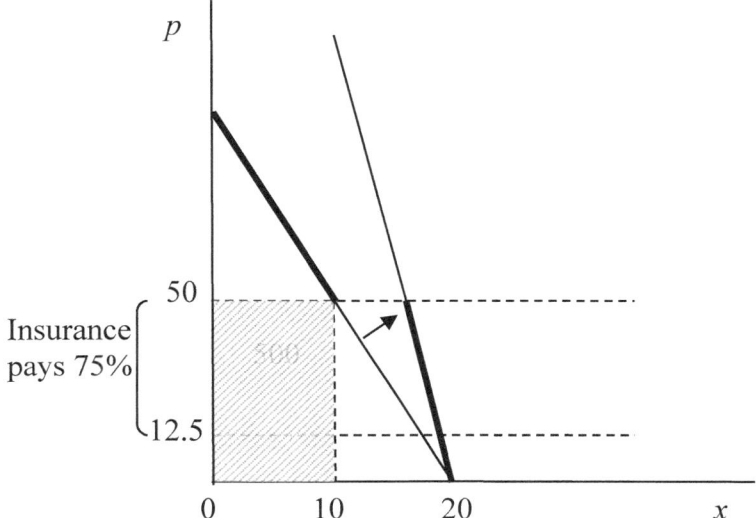

$500 deductible + 25 percent coinsurance

The demand curve rotates outward when $x > 10$ units, i.e., medical expenditure exceeds the deductible ($50 \cdot 10 = 500$). Thus, the new demand curve is represented by a bold line.

b. Now assume the policy does not have a deductible but pays 100 percent of expenses after a stop loss of $2,000. Show this graphically.

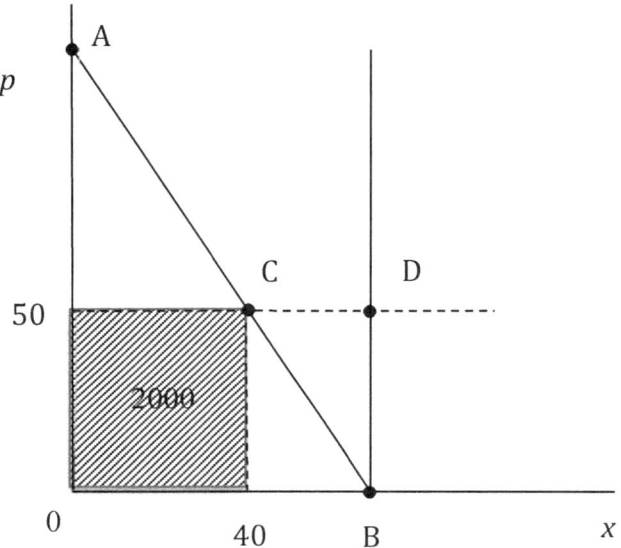

Given that the price of medical care is $50 and the stop loss is $2,000, which means that the patient pays for care up to the point at which the quantity of medical care demanded is 40. Beyond this point, the consumer pays nothing out-of-pocket. Thus, the demand curve is a vertical line at x = B. With the stop loss, quantity demanded increases from 40 to B right after the stop loss is satisfied.

3.7   Explain which of the following types of insurance coverage would more likely cause the most major problems resulting from moral hazard. (If you do not know some of the medical terms, check out Google.com.)

a. indemnity payments of $10,000 for each eye or limb lost or indemnity payments of $50 for each day spent in the nursing home;

An indemnity payment of $50 for each day spent in the nursing home alters the relative price of home care and nursing home care. The price of nursing home care becomes cheaper relative to the price of home care (opportunity cost of caregiver). Thus, elderly individuals have an incentive to use more nursing home care under such coverage. This is called "moral hazard." By contrast, most people have no incentive to intentionally claim indemnity payments of $10,000 for each eye or limb lost. This is because the value borne by the individual of losing an eye or a limb is substantially larger than the indemnity payment.

b. arthroscopic surgery for knee injuries or amputation of the foot;

Knee injuries occur frequently. Thus insurance coverage for arthroscopic surgery is likely to increase use of such surgery because many people may need such surgery.

c. family counseling or electroconvulsive therapy;

In addition to health care cost, people face a higher "price" of using electroconvulsive therapy, such as a loss of memory, as compared to family counseling. Thus, insurance coverage is more likely to increase the use of family counseling than to encourage use of electroconvulsive therapy.

d. decongestants or antibiotics.

This is an empirical question. A fixed dollar subsidy per purchase is likely to increase demand for both.

3.9 **Use the equation for time price given by equation 3.3 in the text to answer the following questions.**

a. Would you expect the elasticity of demand with respect to c to be higher or lower for a business executive than for a day laborer? Explain your answer.

The elasticity of demand with respect to c is lower for business executives than for day laborers because the wage of a business executive is higher than that of a day laborer.

b. Who would be more likely to use a "free clinic" (free in the sense that the money price of services = 0)? Why?

As shown in equation (3.3), the full price of using a "free clinic" includes wt. Suppose that t is the same among patients. Hence, we can infer that day laborers are more likely to use a "free clinic" because the wage of a day laborer is lower than the wage of a business executive.

3.11   Assume there are two drugs designed to treat high blood pressure, drug A and drug B. Blood pressure readings from patients taking drug A are consistently higher than those of patients taking drug B. Does this mean that drug B is more effective than drug A? Why or why not? Describe how a randomized controlled trial could be set up to settle this issue.

We cannot conclude that drug B is more effective than drug A simply because patients taking drug B achieve a better outcome than do patients taking drug A. There is a "sample selection" problem. Users of drugs A and B are not randomly selected. Physicians and patients select drugs A or B for reasons that may be unknown to researchers. For example, young patients may be more likely to select drug B and elder patients may be more likely to select drug A. As a result, the better outcome of drug B may reflect an effect of age rather than efficacy per se.

A randomized control trial often uses a "double-blind" approach to randomly assign patients into two groups: (1) users of drug A; and (2) users of drug B. Assignment to groups is random and not based on health or other factors. In this case, neither patients nor physicians know which type of drugs their patients use.

Chapter 4

Demand for Private Health Insurance

4.1 **Suppose a person is diagnosed with lung cancer. Describe four types of pecuniary losses and two types of nonpecuniary losses that are likely to arise.**

Pecuniary losses include (1) medical cost; (2) paid care cost; (3) earnings loss; and (4) transportation (to provider) cost.

Non-pecuniary losses include (1) pain and suffering associated with the disease and (2) disability, in that patients may lose some ability in daily activities such as walking and lifting heavy objects.

State	Probability (θ)	Income (W)	Utility (U)
Sick	0.4	2,500	$U(2,500)$
Healthy	0.6	4,900	$U(4,900)$

4.3   Based on the same information reported in the above table in exercise 2, calculate the maximum amount that John is willing to pay to avoid the risk of income loss resulting from becoming sick if the probability of becoming sick increases from 0.4 to 0.5. Is John more likely to buy health insurance than he would under conditions specified in exercise 2? Justify your answer by comparing your results for this question with what you obtained in exercise 4.2.

The maximum amount that John is willing to pay to avoid the risk of income loss is $W_w - W_w{'}$, where $W_w = E(W) = (1 - \theta)W_h + \theta W_s$ and $W_{w'}$ is the wealth that satisfies the condition

$EU(W) = U(W_w{'})$. Based on the information given in exercise 4.2:

For Case 1: $W_w = (0.4)(2500) + (0.6)(4900) = 3940$.

$E(U(W)) = (0.4)(2500^{0.5}) + (0.6)(4900^{0.5}) = 20 + 42 = 62$.

Solve: $62 = (W_{w'})^{0.5}$ So $W_{w'} = 3844$.

	Probability of becoming sick	W_w	$W_{w'}$	$W_w - W_{w'}$
Case 1	0.4	3,940	3,844	96
Case 2	0.5	3,700	3,600	100

John is more likely to buy health insurance in case 2 (probability of becoming sick is 0.5) than he would in case 1 because the maximum amount that John is willing to pay to avoid the risk of income loss is higher in case 2 than in case 1.

4.5   Assume that the individual is a risk lover. The individual can purchase a gamble with a 0.01 probability of winning $10,000. Assume the person has an annual income of $10,000. What is the actuarial value of the gamble? Show graphically why the person would rather gamble than not, and explain your answer.

The actuarial value of the gamble is 100 (10,000 × 0.01). We can use the graph shown in figure 4.4 to explain why the person would rather gamble than not gamble. Since the individual is a risk lover, his or her marginal utility of wealth increases with increases in wealth. This means that the expected utility of two uncertain incomes (one outcome is 10,000 minus the price of the lottery [if the individual loses], the other is 20,000 minus the price of the lottery [if the individual wins]) is higher than the utility of a certain income (10,000). Thus, the person is willing to pay more than 100 (the expected gain) for having the opportunity to gamble.

4.7 Considering each of the following pairs, in which of the two is purchase of health insurance more likely? Explain your answers.

a. the rich versus the poor;

Under the assumption that the amount of income loss is fixed among persons and there is no government subsidy for purchasing health insurance, we expect the poor to be more likely to purchase health insurance than the rich because a given loss, e.g., $5,000, generates a higher relative utility loss for the poor than that for the rich person. In practice, the rich are more likely to purchase health insurance than the poor, particularly when the country offers a tax subsidy for the purchase of health insurance like the one in the United States. Another reason may be that the rich purchase more care when they are sick (e.g., stay in a private hospital room).

b. hospital care versus a physician office visit;

Since the demand for health insurance depends on the size of loss, people are more likely to purchase health insurance coverage for hospital care than for physician office visits.

c. a probability of getting sick of 0.95 versus a 0.5 probability of getting sick;

The demand for health insurance is positively associated with the variance of loss. A probability of getting sick of 0.95 has a lower variance than does a probability of getting sick of 0.5. Thus, people are more likely to buy health insurance for a 0.5 probability of getting sick.

d. a tax subsidy (the premium of health insurance is not subject to any form of taxation) versus a tax credit.

In the United States, at present, employer-provided health insurance is subject to an unlimited tax subsidy. Thus at the margin, a dollar of medical care costs the person receiving such benefits $1 -$ marginal tax rate. If a tax credit were fixed at a certain level, above the threshold, the level at which the tax credit is fixed, an extra dollar of health insurance premiums and the medical care paid by the insurance would cost the person a dollar. So demand for health insurance is greater under the tax subsidy.

Chapter 5

The Market for Physicians' Services

5.1   The following two tables are mean physician net income by physician age after expenses and before taxes (in thousands of dollars), by year and by specialty.

Table A. Physician Age and Earnings ($ thous.)

	1973	1974	1975	1977	1978	1979	1981	1982	1983
Physician Age									
Less than 36 years	32.8	40.6	43.7	49.6	49.0	64.3	62.5	73.3	77.0
36–45 years	51.9	57.1	62.9	69.9	70.1	87.5	98.1	100.2	110.2
46–55 years	55.0	58.9	62.3	67.7	76.2	87.1	110.8	116.5	133.6
56–65 years	48.3	49.3	54.1	58.7	65.3	75.9	95.6	99.5	103.1
66 or more years	31.9	34.0	35.0	36.8	44.4	54.9	68.3	64.3	71.9

Table B. Physician Specialty and Earnings ($ thous.)

	Specialty									
	All*	GP/FP	Int. Med.	Surg.	Ped.	Ob./GY	Rad.	Psych.	Anesth.	Path.
Physician Age										
Less than 36 years	77.0	57.9	68.0	108.8	44.7	78.9	100.3	64.9	126.9	90.3
36–45 years	110.2	68.2	95.1	146.3	81.2	118.7	150.1	81.7	146.1	109.9
46–55 years	133.6	77.8	125.4	183.8	81.2	139.4	161.6	90.4	161.3	134.1
56–65 years	103.1	76.4	98.3	120.0	73.6	129.0	171.5	79.0	119.8	141.3
66 or more years	71.9	50.0	75.0	94.8	59.4	89.5	—	62.1	—	—

Notes: * Includes physicians in specialties not listed separately. Abbreviations: GP/FP, general practitioner/family practitioner; Int. Med., internal medicine; Surg., surgery; Ped., pediatrics; Ob./Gyn., obstetrics/gynecology; Rad., radiology; Psych., psychiatry; Anesth., anesthesiology; and Path., pathology.

Based on data reported in these two tables, compute the present value of a medical education, assuming a 3 percent real discount rate.

You need to assume an age at which the medical career begins and the age at which the doctor will retire. Assume the career begins at age 32 and ends at age 65. Then using data from the 1973 column as an example, assume 32.8 is for less than age 34, and set earnings for each of the other age groups at the midpoint of the age category. Linearly interpolate values for the other years and calculate the present value using a 3% discount rate.

5.3   Suppose the country's national health insurance authority cuts the price it pays physicians for performing a procedure. Use a goods-leisure analysis (goods or income on one axis and leisure on the other) to answer the following questions:

a. A backward-bending supply curve of labor can be derived from the indifference curve analysis of goods and leisure. Explain using graphs (one for the indifference curve analysis and the other for the supply of labor function corresponding to the indifference curve analysis).

A backward-bending supply curve of labor can be derived from the following two figures. In panel A the line TA represents a budget constraint which in turn describes all possible combinations between leisure hours and consumption goods given wage (w) and total time available to the individual (T). Indifference curves are represented by I; such curves describe all possible combination of consumption goods and leisure hours that yield the same level of utility to the individual. The individual's optimal choice is determined at the point of tangency between budget line and the indifference curve, e.g., at E_1. At E_1, the optimal leisure number hours is l_0 and the optimal number of leisure hours is l_0 and optimal hours of work (labor supply) is $T - l_0$. Panel B shows the labor supply curve where the horizontal axis represents work hours and the vertical axis represents wage levels. In panel A, the individual supplies $T - l_0$ hours of work when the wage level is at w_1, as shown in the point E_1.

As the wage level increases, such as from w_1 to w_2, the budget line rotates outward, implying that individuals can purchase more consumption goods than previously when they allocate some of their time to work. In panel A, the new equilibrium point is at E_2, indicating that the individual will devote more hours to work. That is, work hours increase from $T - l_0$ to $T - l_1$. Thus, panel B shows that the labor supply curve has a positive slope, between the points of E_1 to E_2. If the wage level continues to increase, such as from w_2 to w_3, there is a new equilibrium point at E_3. In this case, the individual reduces the work hours from $T - l_1$ to $T - l_2$. Thus, in panel B, the labor supply curve has a negative slope between E_2 and E_3. Work hours decrease as the wage level increases over this range. This is because the income effect dominates the substitution effect as wages increase at a relatively high level.

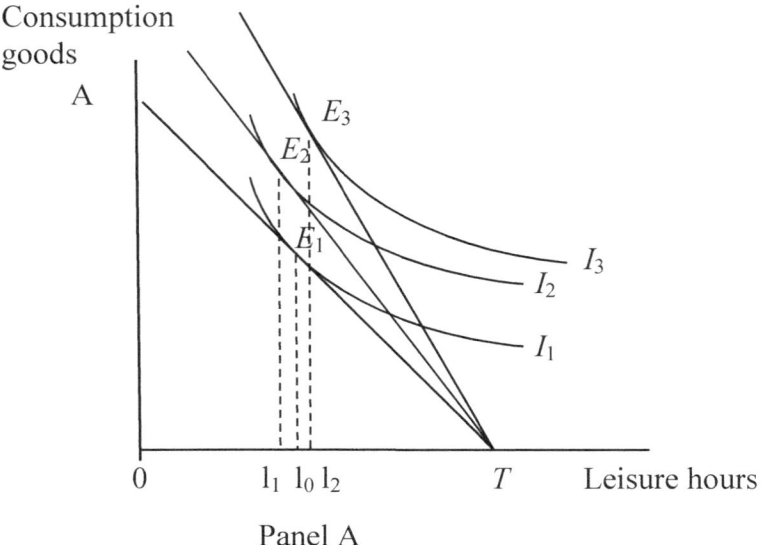

Panel A

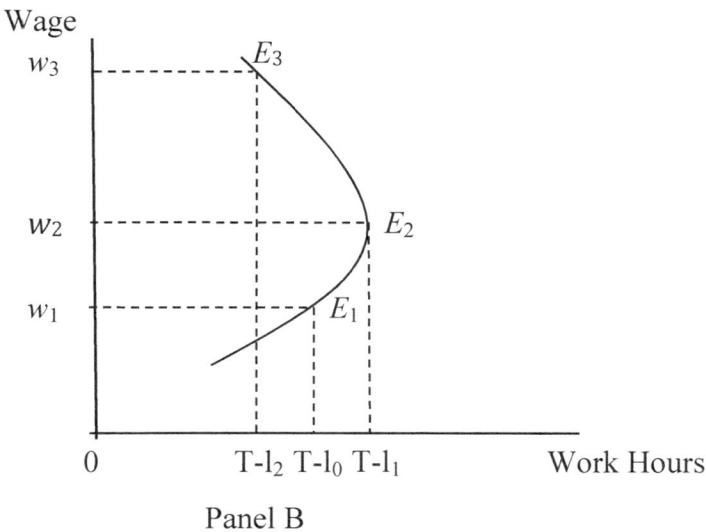

Panel B

A backward-bending supply curve of labor

b. Isolate income and substitution effects from a decrease in the wage rate. (*Note:* In isolating the income and substitution effect, the practice is to draw a line parallel to the new price line and tangent to the indifference curve where the person was *before* the price change.)

The decomposition of the income and substitution effects can be shown by the figure below. At the original wage level, the budget line is AT. The equilibrium point is represented by E_0, a point of tangency between the budget line and the indifference curve I_0. As the wage decreases, the budget line rotates inward, from AT to BT. The new equilibrium point at E_1, indicating that the individual decreases hours of work as the wage level decreases. We now decompose this effect into two parts: (1) a substitution effect; and (2) an income effect. The substitution effect represents the pure effect of the change in relative price, holding real income constant. To show this effect, we draw a "virtual" budget line parallel to the new budget line; this virtual line is tangent at E_2 to the "old" indifference curve I_0. The move from E_1 to E_2 is the pure effect of the change in wage holding "real income" constant. Since the slope of the indifference curve is downward sloping, the substitution effect is always negative; the individual increases hours of leisure as the wage decreases.

By contrast, the income effect represents the effect of change in real income holding the relative price of leisure (the wage rate) constant. The income effect is the difference in work hours between l_2 to l_1. The income effect is always positive as long as leisure is a "normal" good. Thus, the individual decreases the leisure hours (from l_2 to l_1) as the wage decreases.

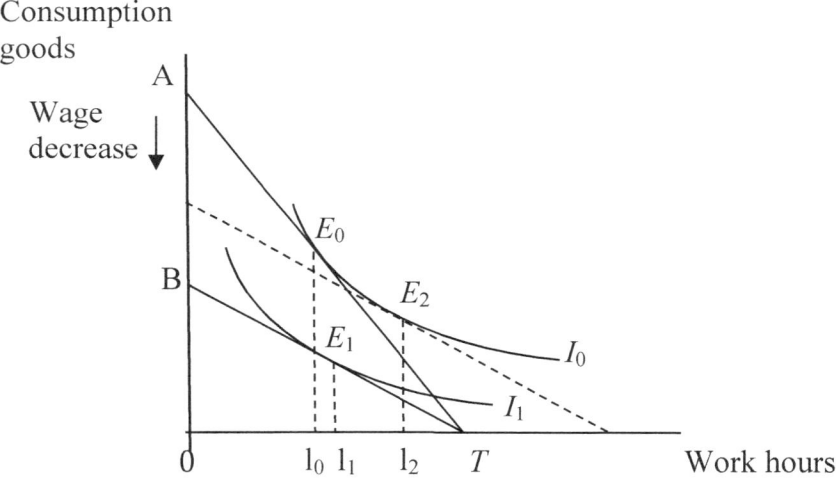

Substitution effect: $E_0 \rightarrow E_2$ ($w\downarrow \rightarrow$ leisure$\uparrow$) Income effect: $E_2 \rightarrow E_1$ ($w\downarrow \rightarrow$ leisure$\downarrow$)

Net effect: $E_0 \rightarrow E_1$ ($w\downarrow \rightarrow$ leisure$\uparrow$) in this graph. Results will differ depending on how the indifference curves are drawn.

c. Now assume that Medicare is the only payer. Medicare decreases the unit price of a service from \$34 to \$24. Show how the goods-leisure analysis is useful for addressing this question. (You will need to translate price per unit of service into work hours. Just make an assumption and state what it is.)

We can treat the unit price of health care services as the wage rate if we set the time required by the physicians to provide a unit of service to 1, e.g., 1 hour. We can then treat the fee reduction from \$34 to \$24 as a decrease in the wage. From the substitution effect, physicians will reduce the volume of their services by reducing the number of work hours. This is because the wage level can be treated as the price of leisure. As the wage decreases, leisure becomes cheaper as compared to going to work. Thus, the physician will substitute leisure for work. By contrast, the income effect is to increase the hours of work (or decrease leisure hours as the wage decreases) by increasing the volume of health care services they provide. If the substitution effect dominates the income effect, physicians will respond to a fee cut by reducing the volume of their services, which corresponds to a positively sloped labor supply curve. By contrast, physicians will respond to fee cut by increasing the volume of their services if the income effect dominates the substitution effect. Then the labor supply curve has a negative slope.

5.5   In 1988, Medicare cut the payment for open-heart surgery by 2–15 percent. Answer the following questions:

a. For thoracic surgeons, who perform open heart surgery, what is the income effect of this fee cut?

The income effect is to increase volume of open-heart surgery to compensate for the income loss from the price reduction.

b. What is the substitution effect induced by this fee cut, again for thoracic surgeons?

The substitution effect is to reduce the volume of service when price is reduced.

c. What happens when the income effect dominates the substitution effect? Does an insurer realize savings from a fee cut when the income effect dominates the substitution effect? Explain your answer. Suppose you were director of your country's national health insurance program. What public policies would you implement if you knew that the income effect dominates the substitution effect?

Physicians will respond to a fee reduction by increasing the volume of their services when the income effect dominates the substitution effect. In this case, an insurer does not completely realize a saving from a fee cut because physicians increase the volume of their services to recoup their revenue loss. If I were the director of a country's NHI program, I would not implement a fee cut because this may be an ineffective tool for controlling cost. If I had no other choice, I would take the volume offset into account in the setting of fee schedule. For example, I would implement a fee cut by 20% when the goal of cost control is to cut fee by 10% if the best available evidence shows that physicians can recoup 50% of their revenue loss through a volume offset.

Chapter 6

Hospitals

6.1 Hospitals are thought to be subject to economies and diseconomies of scale and scope. What is meant by economies (diseconomies) of scale and scope? What are sources of scale economies (diseconomies) and scope economies (diseconomies) in hospital settings? List and discuss up to three each for scale and scope economies.

Economies of scale indicate that hospitals' average cost decreases as output increases. By contrast, diseconomies of scale indicate that hospitals' average cost increases as output increases. Economies of scope means that the average cost is lower if the hospital provides two or more services (such as neurology and psychiatry) than if the hospital only provides one service (only providing psychiatry). Diseconomies of scope mean that provision of several services by a single hospital is less efficient (in terms of average cost) than having each hospital specialize in the provision of a single service. We list possible sources of scale economies (diseconomies) and scope economies (diseconomies) in hospitals below:

	Sources
Economies of scale	1. Lower average fixed cost of equipment: larger hospitals have an advantage in having lower average fixed cost per unit of service for providing advanced technologies, such as MRI. 2. Reduce variable cost: larger hospitals have more bargaining power in negotiating acquisition prices of various forms of medical inputs and supplies. 3. Reduce average labor cost: Labor employed by hospitals is very heterogeneous in the sense that one type of labor, such as nurses, is not a perfect substitute for other types of labor, such as medical examiners working in a laboratory. Larger hospitals have an advantage to reduce average labor cost because they hire larger numbers of each category of health professionals.

Diseconomies of scale	1. Larger hospitals may face a higher risk of patient infection. Thus, larger hospitals may invest more in the infection control than smaller hospitals do. 2. Larger hospitals may need to set up a system to monitor hospital activities which in turn requires a high overhead cost. 3. Medical staffs in larger hospitals may need to spend more effort and time to communicate in order to assure that the treatment task has been done appropriately. This in turn may reduce the efficiency of hospital operations.
Economies of scope	1. There may be spillovers from provision of one service to others. For example, a heart surgery program may improve the quality of emergency room care. 2. Hospitals can lower average fixed cost for the investment in infrastructure in the hospitals such as information and communication systems if hospitals offer two or more types of services.
Diseconomies of scope	1. Hospitals offering two or more types of services may create competition for the time and effort of hospital administrators.

	2. Hospitals offering two or more types of service may need to set a special unit to coordinate the inputs used in the different departments. The increase in the overhead cost for such a unit may outweigh the benefits to hospitals of offering several different types of services.
	3. Hospitals offering too many types of services may not realize an efficiency gain from the "division of labor" because hospitals may lose the advantage of specialization. It may be advisable to deliver fewer types of services at a higher volume than more services at a lower volume per type of service. For one, a higher volume facilitates "learning by doing."

6.3 Now assume that the hospital is a monopolist with a demand function that incorporates quality of care as well as quantity. Quality enters into both the demand and cost functions according to $p = 100 - 3x + 4\sqrt{y}$ and $C = 4x^2 + 10x + y$, where p is the price of hospital care, x is the quantity of hospital care, y is the quality of hospital care, and C is total cost. Compute the hospital's profit-maximizing output, quality, price, revenue, and profit.

Let π represent the profit function. Then
$\pi = p \cdot x - C = (100 - 3x + 4\sqrt{y}) \cdot x - (4x^2 + 10x + y) = 90x - 7x^2 + 4x\sqrt{y} - y$.
The hospital chooses the optimal x and y to maximize the profit.

This is solved from the following two first-order conditions:
$\partial\pi/\partial x = 90 - 14x + 4\sqrt{y} = 0$ and $\partial\pi/\partial y = 2x/\sqrt{y} - 1 = 0$.

By solving these two equations simultaneously, we obtain $x = 15$, and $y = 900$. Substituting these two values in the price and profit functions, we obtain $p = 175$ and $\pi = 675$.

6.5   As described in the chapter, in Newhouse's model, the hospital maximizes utility, which depends on levels of quantity and quality of care, subject to a break-even constraint (price equals average cost). Use this model to analyze the effects of the following exogenous changes in the hospital's production possibility curve—that is, the hospital quantity-quality frontier (as shown in fig. 6.3)—and the hospital's optimal choices of quantity and quality of care (as shown in fig. 6.4).

a. an increase in the wage rate paid to the hospital's employees;

An increase in the wage rate paid to the hospital's employees shifts its average cost curve upward, which in turn shifts the hospital's production possibility curve inward. As a result, the hospital's decision maker faces a less favorable quantity-quality trade-off (curve shifts inward).

b. an increase in the number of persons with health insurance coverage in the hospital's market area;

An increase in the number of persons with health insurance coverage in the hospital's market area leads to an increase in the market demand for hospital care at each quality level, which in turn shifts the hospital's production possibility curve outward. This implies a more favorable quantity-quality trade-off for the hospital decision maker.

c. implementation of a fixed dollar subsidy per unit of hospital care by the city government.

If the hospital is the recipient of the government subsidy of hospital care, then a fixed dollar subsidy per unit of hospital care leads to a decrease in the average cost curve, which in turn shifts the hospital's production possibility curve outward.

6.7   In some settings, physicians are employed on a fixed salary basis by the hospital. In others, physicians function as independent entrepreneurs and bill for care they deliver to hospitalized patients separately from the hospital's bill for its services. Describe three differences that you would expect to arise under these distinct employment/compensation arrangements for physicians.

As shown in the following table, we answer this question in terms of effects on: (1) quantity; (2) quality; and (3) cost.

	Physicians function as employees of hospitals and receive fixed salaries	Physicians function as independent entrepreneurs
Quantity	Since earnings are not dependent on the number of patients, physicians have no incentive to provide a quantity of care, which is larger than the required level. For example, physicians do not take a quick lunch to see extra patients.	Since the physicians' earnings depend on the number of patients seen, the physician has an incentive to see more patients.

Quality	Physicians have no financial incentive to provide a quality level that is higher than the minimum acceptable level.	Physicians have an incentive to provide higher quality of care to increase demand for their care.
Cost	Physicians have no direct incentive to care about the hospital's cost.	Physicians have no direct incentive to save on cost because the saving accrues to the hospital.

6.9 **Assume there is only one hospital in a small town. This hospital faces a demand function given by $p = 304 - 2x$, where p is the price of hospital care and x is the quantity of hospital care, and a cost function given by $C = 500 + 4x + 8x^2$, where C is total cost.**

a. Suppose the local government imposes a price regulation on hospitals that sets the price of hospital care at 250. Show the effects of this price ceiling on the hospital's quantity of care and its revenue and profit. Be sure to indicate what the values of quantity, revenue, and profit would be in the absence of such regulation.

Let π represent the profit function. Then
$$\pi = p \cdot x - C = (304 - 2x) \cdot x - (500 + 4x + 8x^2) = 300x - 10x^2 - 500.$$

If there is no government regulation, the hospital chooses the optimal x to maximize profit. This first order condition is:

   $d\pi/dx = 300 - 20x = 0.$

Thus, $x = 15$, $p = 304 - (2 \cdot 15) = 274$, and $\pi = 1{,}750$.

Under this government regulation, the regulatory body sets price at 250. Then the hospital will set quantity of care at $x = 27$, which is calculated by substituting $p = 250$ into the demand function.

Total revenue is 6,750 and total cost is 6,440. Thus, $\pi =$ 6,750 – 6,440 = 310. The effect of government regulation can be seen using the following table:

	Price	Quantity	Revenue	Cost	Profit
Without regulation	274	15	4,110	2,360	1,750
With price regulation at $p = 250$	250	27	6,750	6,440	310

The price ceiling increases the quantity of hospital care and revenue, but it reduces the profit earned by the hospital.

b. If the local government were to further lower the maximum price that the hospital can charge to patients to 240, compute the effect of this new price ceiling on the hospital's quantity of care and its revenue and profit, compared to the older, higher price ceiling. Will this hospital remain in the market or will it exit? Explain your answer.

Using the same reasoning, we obtain the following table when the price ceiling is set at 240:

	Price	Quantity	Revenue	Cost	Profit
With price regulation at $p = 240$	240	32	7,680	8,820	−1,140

The quantity of hospital care will increase as the regulator reduces price further; profit will further decrease and become negative. That is, cost exceeds revenue that the hospital receives. Although the hospital runs a deficit, the hospital may not exit the market if the regulated price exceeds the average variable cost. If so, the hospital can recoup part of the fixed cost by keeping the hospital in business. Variable cost is cost that varies with quantity of hospital care. Thus, total variable cost (TVC) is $4x + 8x^2$. Since average variable cost (AVC) = TVC/x, $AVC = 4 + 8x$. Based on this function, $AVC = 260$ when $x = 32$. AVC is greater than the regulated price (240). Thus, such regulation will force the hospital to exit from the market.

Chapter 7

Quality of Care and Medical Malpractice

7.1 Suppose a physician receives a fixed payment ($\hat{p}$) for providing health care services to a patient and there is a probability of the patient incurring iatrogenic injury (θ) that causes monetary loss to the patient ($\hat{L}$). Assume that the patient's monetary loss is fixed once the injury has occurred. However, the probability of injury depends on the physician's level of care (e for effort). That is, $\theta = \theta(e)$. The probability of injury decreases as the level of physician care increases (i.e., $\theta'(e) < 0$). In addition, the effort involved in increasing the level of care is costly to the physician in terms of time, stress, and nonphysician inputs the physician employs in his or her practice. Thus, the physician faces a cost function C, which also depends on the level of care. $C = C(e)$. $C'(e) > 0$; cost increases with the level of care. Using this information, answer the following questions.

a. Assume that the physician's sole objective in practicing medicine is to maximize profit, list the physician's objective (profit) function under the following liability regimes: (i) no liability, (ii) strict liability, and (iii) negligence liability.

Let S represent physician's revenue (or sales).

	The physician's objective (profit) function
no liability	$S - C(e)$
strict liability	$S - C(e) - \theta(e)\hat{L}$
negligence	$S - C(e)$ if $e \geq e*$
liability	$S - C(e) - \theta(e)\hat{L}$ if $e < e*$

b. With the level of care (e) on the horizontal axis and the profit ($) on the vertical axis, show graphically how the physician determines the optimal level of care under each of the three alternative liability regimes.

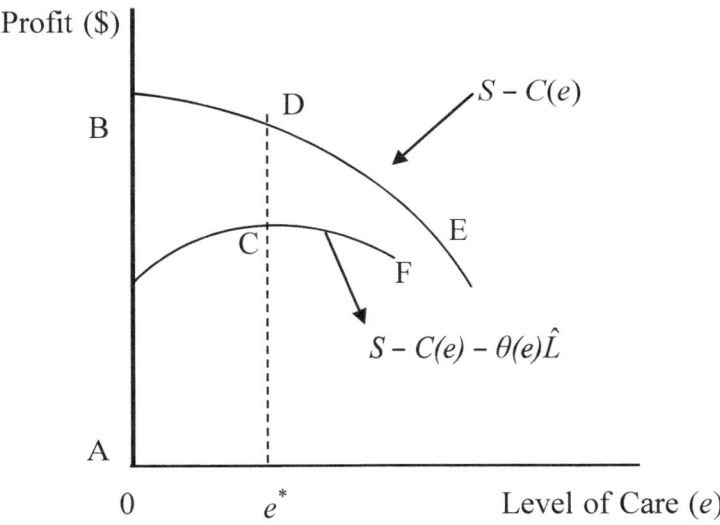

No liability: The optimal level of care = 0 because profit reaches its maximum point at $e = 0$ (point B).

Strict liability: The optimal level of care = e^* because profit reaches its maximum point at $e = e^*$ (at point C).

Negligence liability: The optimal level of care = e^* if the court sets the due care standard at e^*.

c. Use a graph similar to figure 7.1 to show how to decide what the socially optimal level of care is.

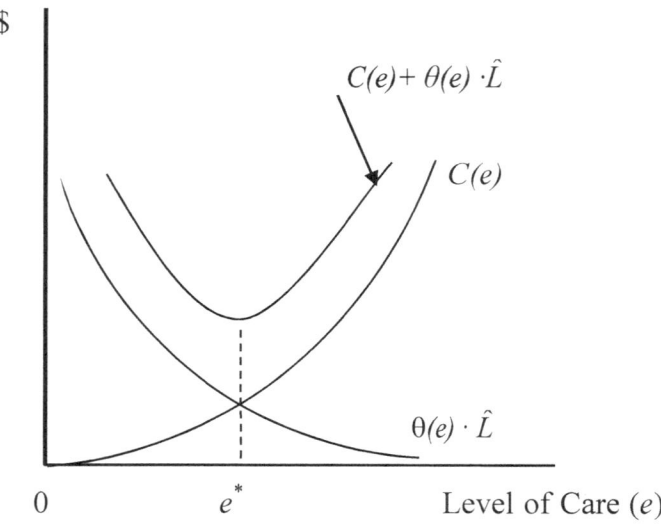

Total social cost for injury prevention is: $C(e) + \theta(e) \cdot \hat{L}$. The socially optimal level of care is the care level that minimizes total social cost (e^*) which is determined by: $C'(e) = -\theta'(e) \cdot \hat{L}$.

d. If the court has sufficient information to set the compensation ($\hat{D}$) equal to the injury victim's monetary loss ($\hat{L}$), which liability rules can ensure that the physician's optimal care level and the socially optimal care level coincide? Explain your answer.

If $D = \hat{L}$, the physician's optimal care level and the socially optimal care level will coincide under strict liability. If the court sets the due care standard at the socially optimal care level, the physician's optimal care level and the socially optimal care level will also coincide under negligence liability.

e. Using a graph, explain the distinction between strict liability and the negligence rule. Under what condition do we expect that these liability rules will achieve the same level of optimal care?

As shown in the graph illustrated under part b, the profit function is the curve ACF under strict liability. In this case, physicians choose the optimal care level at the point where expected profit reaches its maximum. By contrast, the profit function is described by two discontinuous parts: curve AC if $e < e^*$ and curve DE if $e \geq e^*$. In this case, expected profit reaches its maximum at care level e^*. Thus, strict liability and negligence liability will achieve the same level of optimal care if the court sets the level of due care at e^*.

7.3   In recent years, many organizations around the world have published rankings of both universities and hospitals. For example, the *U.S. News and World Report* has regularly published "The Top 10 Best Universities in the US" and "the Top 10 Best Hospitals in the US" for many years.

a. What are likely to be differences between the hospital ranking and the university ranking in terms of their information content? Which one is likely to provide more valid and reliable information for potential users? Why is this so?

Considering three dimensions of quality: structure; process; and outcome. In higher education, the outcome (student performance) depends on students' effort as well as professors' effort. By contrast, the outcome of health care is often less dependent on patients' efforts. As a result, university rankings consist mostly of information on the structure of higher education, such as the quality or reputations of professors, rather than on information on student outcomes. By contrast, a hospital ranking may be useful if the ranking contains information on patient outcomes. However, patient health improves or fails to improve for many idiosyncratic reasons. Careful adjustment for patient severity of illness is needed to generate valid indicators of patient outcomes. Thus, university rankings provide more valid and reliable information for potential users than do hospital rankings based on patient outcome measures.

b. Would you expect there to be any difference between private and public agencies in performing rankings of hospitals? Suppose both a private firm and a public agency were to publish a "10 Best Hospitals" list for the city where you live. Which organization's ranking would be more valuable to probable hospital patients? Justify your answer.

Since information on health care quality is a public good, and data assembly and adjustment can be very expensive, private agencies have no incentive to perform the hospital ranking unless the rankings are profitable, such as increasing sales of magazines. Thus, private agencies face a trade-off. On the one hand, they have an incentive to increase the quality of their rankings because a good ranking report could be financially beneficial. On the other hand, they also have incentives to cut cost in data assembly and checking for errors, which may reduce the credibility of the ranking. Since potential hospital patients may not have enough information to evaluate the quality of hospital rankings, private agencies may have a stronger incentive to cut cost than to improve quality. Thus, a ranking report by a public agency may be more valuable to potential hospital patients if the public agencies have sufficient funding to prepare a credible hospital ranking report.

c. List the pros and cons of hospital rankings from the viewpoint of the consumer.

Hospital rankings can promote health care quality if the rankings provide valid and reliable information. However, given that the patient selection process can affect the outcomes at particular hospitals, rankings should be adjusted for case mix. In addition, hospitals may respond to the prospect of being ranked by selecting healthy patients. This may create a cycle in which hospitals are constantly attempting to improve their measured outcomes by selecting increasingly healthier patients to be one step ahead of the adjustment process.

d. How would you expect hospitals to respond to published hospital rankings? Is there any evidence to support your argument?

As just mentioned, hospitals may respond strategically to hospital rankings by selecting healthier patients. Dranove et al. (2003) find evidence that reports on quality of hospital care led hospitals to select healthier patients who are more likely to survive a surgical procedure.

7.5   In table 7.1, we list four incentive mechanisms (professional norms, regulation, market competition, and tort law) for ensuring high levels of health care quality.

a. Among these four mechanisms, which one seems to play a relatively more important role in your country? Explain your answer.

This answer is country-specific. Consider the case of China: more than 90% of hospitals in China are public and heavily regulated by the government. In addition, entry of private hospitals is rare due to strict regulation, which in turn, limits the role of market competition in enhancing quality of care. Furthermore, the legal system in China is inadequate for resolving medical disputes and related quality of care problems. This suggests that regulation plays a relatively more important role in assuring quality of health care in China than in countries in which potential entry of competitors provides a disincentive for existing hospitals to offer low quality care.

b. Do the four mechanisms listed in table 7.1 also ensure high quality levels for higher education (university)? Why or why not?

Except for tort law, the mechanisms listed in table 7.1 also play important roles in assuring high quality levels for higher education. Universities are rarely defendants in legal disputes.

c. Medical malpractice claims (i.e., patients suing their physicians and/or hospitals) are fairly common in many countries. Is it common for students to sue their university professors for a suboptimal quality of teaching? Can you conceive of tort law being used as mechanism for ensuring a high quality of higher education? Why or why not?

Low quality of medical care may result in personal injury or death. Thus, patients and/or their families use tort law to sue their doctors or hospitals. By contrast, the low quality of higher education will not directly result in personal injury or death. Thus, it is much more difficult to demonstrate that a student suffered a considerable loss from poor quality teaching at a university.

Chapter 8

Nurses in Hospital and Long-Term Care Services

8.1   The Good Works General Hospital has a local monopoly in the sale of hospital services in its market area. Its product demand curve is $p = 30 - 0.4x$, where p is the price of a hospital day and x is the number of hospital days per year at Good Works. Given this demand curve, derive the equation for marginal revenue (MR).

Good Works is the only employer of professional nurses in its market area. It faces a supply of nurse labor of $w = 5 + 0.9E$, where w is the nurse hourly wage and E is the full- time-equivalent of nurses employed by Good Works. What is the marginal labor cost of nurses? Assume each nurse can monitor four patient rooms per hour (with one patient per room) and Good Works is a profit maximizer. Then how many professional nurses should Good Works employ? At what hourly wage? What price should Good Works charge for a hospital day?

Total revenue (TR) $= p \cdot x = (30 - 0.4x) \cdot x = 30x - 0.4x^2$.

Marginal revenue (MR) $= \dfrac{dTR}{dx} = 30 - 0.8x$

Total factor (labor) cost (TFC) $= w \cdot E = (5 + 0.9) \cdot E = 5E + 0.9E^2$.

Marginal factor (labor) cost (MFC) $= \dfrac{dTFC}{dE} = 5 + 1.8E$.

As shown in fig. 8.4, the profit-maximizing hospital determines the optimal number of nurses (labor) by setting MRP = MFC, where MRP $= \dfrac{dTRP}{dE}$ and TRP = total revenue product. In this question, we assume each nurse can monitor 4 patient rooms per hour; this implies $x = 4E$. Substituting this relationship into TR,

TRP $= 120E - 6.4E^2$. Then, we obtain MRP $= \dfrac{dTRP}{dE} = 120 - 12.8E$.

Since MRP = MFC, we solve for the optimal E by using the following equation:

$5 + 1.8E = 120 - 12.8E.$

Thus, $E = \dfrac{115}{14.6} = 7.88$. Then we obtain $w = 12.09$ when $E = 7.88$ through the supply curve of nurse labor ($w = 5 + 0.9E$). With $E = 7.88$, $x = 4 \cdot 7.88 = 31.52$. Substituting $x = 31.52$ into demand curve ($p = 30 - 0.4x$), $p = 17.39$.

8.3 Consider the community (city or town) in which you live. Are local hospitals likely to be monopsonists? Why or why not?

We use the following two cases to determine whether a local hospital is likely to be monopsonist.

Description of the hypothetical community	Explanation
A large metropolitan area: there are more than 10 hospitals within the urban and suburban area.	The wage of nurse is determined by market forces (demand and supply). The individual hospital is less likely to be a wage setter, but rather a wage taker. In addition, the nurses are mobile because they can easily move from one hospital to another. Thus, a local hospital in this large city is less likely to possess monopsony power in the nurse labor market.
A small city in a remote area: there is only one hospital in the city and surrounding area.	The local hospital is the single buyer and mobility of nurses is limited. Thus, it is highly likely that the local hospital will possess power in the nurse labor market.

8.5   Following the concept of full price in exercise 11 of chapter 3, let Y represent full income, where Y = wage income + nonwage income.

a. Would you expect the elasticity of labor supply with respect to wage to be higher or lower for a nurse with a higher share of nonwage income than for a nurse with a lower share of nonwage income? Explain your answer in total income.

As seen in the solution to exercises 5.3 and 5.5, the response of labor supply (hours of work) with respect to a change in the wage can be decomposed into two effects: (1) a substitution effect; and (2) an income effect. The substitution effect indicates the pure effect of the change in price of leisure. The substitution effect leads the individual to increase hours of leisure (i.e., decrease hours of work) as the wage decreases. By contrast, the income effect represents the effect of change in real income holding the relative price of leisure (wage level) constant. The income effect leads the individual to decrease the number of leisure hours (i.e., increase hours of work) as the wage decreases. Since these two effects operate in the opposite directions, we can expect that the wage elasticity (the response of labor supply with respect to the change in wage level) is smaller when the offsetting income effect is larger. Hence, we predict that a nurse with a higher share of nonwage income in total household income is likely to have a lower wage elasticity than a nurse with a lower share of nonwage income because the income effect is likely to be larger for the former than the latter.

b. Based on your answer to (a), would you expect the elasticity of labor supply with respect to wage to be higher or lower for a "female profession" (such as nursing) compared to a "male profession" (such as a pilot), other things being equal? Explain your answer.

Based on the same reasoning, a female professional is likely to have a lower wage elasticity than a male professional because nonwage income is likely to represent a higher share of total household income for female than that male professionals. A husband's wage income acts as nonwage income to the wife's and vice versa. There is a counterargument, however. To the extent that women are more likely to be caregivers of children and elderly parents, the substitution effect may be stronger for women. If so, the elasticity of labor supply may be higher (more positive) for women than for men.

8.7 Suppose the aggregate demand curve for nurses in an island city is $N^d = 300 - 5w$, where w is the hourly wage rate for nurses and N^d is the number of nurses demanded in this city. The supply of nurses is $N^s = 5w - 100$, where N^s is the number of nurses supplied to market. In addition, the city government publicly announces that the city needs to hire 125 nurses in order to provide good-quality hospital care to its citizens. Meanwhile, the city government regulates the wage rate for nurses at $w = 30$.

Answer the following questions:

a. Use both economic and need-based approaches to calculate the nursing shortage under the current regulated wage rate. Do these two approaches yield the same estimates on the number of nursing shortage?

The market equilibrium wage is determined at the intersection of demand and supply curves. Thus, we solve the equilibrium wage from $N^d = N^s$. That is, $300 - 5w = 5w - 100$. $w = 40$ from this equation. At $w = 40$, $N^d = N^s = 100$.

The city government sets the wage at 30, which is less than the market-clearing wage. The wage clears $N^d = 150$ and $N^s = 50$ at this wage. Thus, there is excess demand (nursing shortage) using the economic approach. Excess demand $= N^d - N^s = 150 - 50 = 100$. However, the nurse shortage is equal to 75 (125 − 50) using the needs-based approach. Thus, these two approaches yield the same conclusion that there is a nursing shortage at the current regulated wage. However, these two approaches yield different estimates of the magnitude of the nursing shortage.

b. If the city government decides to recruit nurses from overseas and this policy shifts the supply of nurse to $N^{s'} = 5w - 50$, does this policy solve the problem of a nursing shortage or just mitigate the extent of a nursing shortage? Does your answer differ according to different definitions of "shortage"? Explain your answer.

If the wage is set at 30, then the $N^{s'} = 100$. Since $N^{s'}$ is still less than N^d at $w = 30$ (150) or the number of nurses determined by the need-based approach (125), this policy only mitigates the extent of a nursing shortage but does not completely eliminate it. This answer is not dependent on the approach used to define the nursing shortage.

c. If the city government further announces raising the wage rate for nurses from 30 to 40 and the policy that allows recruiting nurses from overseas remains valid, does the city government solve the problem of nursing shortage or create a new problem? Does your answer differ according to different definitions of "shortage"? Explain your answer.

If the regulated wage is set at 40, $N^d = 100$, but $N^{s'} = 150$. Since $N^{s'}$ is greater than N^d and the number of nurses needed ($N = 125$), there is a nurse surplus. That is, under both approaches, there is a nurse surplus instead of nurse shortage under the new policy.

Chapter 9

Pharmaceutical Manufacturers

9.1 **Suppose that the demand function of a pharmaceutical firm is $p = 20 - 0.5x$, where p is the price of a prescription drug and x is the number of prescription drugs demanded by patients. For simplicity, assume that the pharmaceutical firm can produce an extra pill at a constant cost, and hence the marginal cost function is $MC = 4$.**

a. Compute the optimal price and quantity for the pharmaceutical firm if the firm receives patent protection from the government.

The optimal price for the firm is set where MR = MC. In this question,

$$\text{TR} = p \cdot x = (20 - 0.5x) \cdot x = 20x - 0.5x^2.$$

$$\text{MR} = \frac{dTR}{dx} = 20 - x.$$

Thus, $x = 16$ from the condition that $20 - x = 4$. Then $p = 12$ when $x = 16$.

b. Assuming that generic competition will drive down the price to marginal cost, compute the quantity of this product demanded when the patent expires.

This means that $p = MC$ after patent expiration. Substituting $p = 20 - 0.5x$, $x = 32$ and $p = 4$.

c. Based on your answer, calculate the welfare loss that the patent system imposes on this product.

The welfare loss $= (\Delta p \cdot \Delta x)/2$ where Δp is the difference between monopoly price and competitive equilibrium price, and Δx is the difference between monopoly quantity and competitive equilibrium quantity. Thus the welfare loss is $[(12 - 4) \cdot (32 - 16)]/2 = 64$.

9.3   Use equation 9.1 to indicate which of the following prescription drugs are likely to receive relatively high advertising budgets from their parent pharmaceutical companies: Explain your answers.

- **new branded drugs for treating a chronic disease;**

- **new branded drugs for treating an acute disease;**

- **off-patent branded drugs for treating a chronic disease;**

- **generic drugs.**

As noted in this chapter, the ratio of the optimal advertising expenditure to sales is positively related to the advertising elasticity of demand, but is negatively related to the absolute value of the price elasticity of demand. Compared to drugs for treating an acute disease, drugs for treating chronic diseases are more likely to have a larger advertising elasticity of demand. Since new branded drugs have fewer competitors than off-patent name brand and generic drugs, the absolute value of the price elasticity of demand tends to be lower for new name brand drugs. Thus, manufacturers of new branded drugs for treating chronic diseases are more likely to spend a larger share of their sales on advertising.

9.5   Some researchers argue that pharmacogenomics (PG), which is the science of using genomic markers to predict drug response, can substantially reduce expected drug development costs through increasing the probability of technical success, requiring shorter clinical development times, and requiring smaller clinical trials. Based on the analytic framework described by figure 9.1, what would you expect the impact of PG on R&D investment by pharmaceutical manufacturers to be?

The decrease in development costs implies an increase in the marginal efficiency of investment, which in turn leads to an increase in the optimal amount of R&D investment by pharmaceutical firms, according to the framework underlying fig. 9.1.

Chapter 10

The Supply of Private Health Insurance

10.1   Define the profit function of the private insurer in the line of health insurance. That is, what are the revenues and costs of the insurance firm?

By definition, total profit = total revenue-total expense. Total revenue of private insurers includes two components: (1) premium revenue (revenue from the sale of insurance); and (2) investment revenue (revenue from investments such as on fixed income (interest-bearing) securities). Total expense also consists of two components: (1) payments in the form of reimbursement for the insured's medical expenditure; and (2) other expenses, including the expenses for processing claims, marketing, and managing investments.

Based on your definition, analyze the effects of the following exogenous changes on the insurer's profit:

a. an increase in interest rate;

An increase in the interest rate will increase investment revenue which in turn increases the insurer's profit, if all else remains constant. Premiums will decline, all other factors held constant.

b. an increase in the insurer's share price in the stock market;

An increase in the insurer's share price in the stock market also increases retained earning and hence internal funds for investment.

c. a general increase in health care expenditures;

A general increase in health care expenditures leads to an increased loss, in turn leading to a decrease in the insurer's profit. Subsequently, premiums will increase and profit will return to its equilibrium level.

d. an increase in population size;

An increase in population expands insurance market size. That is, market demand for private health insurance will increase as population size increases. If there is no new entry of insurers, then the premium revenue per insurer will increase, leading to an increase in the insurer's profit. But in the long-run, entry of other insurers is likely to occur.

e. an increase in the country's unemployment rate;

Assume that health insurance is offered through place of employment. Then an increase in the country's unemployment rate leads to a decrease in the number of employees. The insurer's profit will consequently decrease as premium revenue and insurer administrative fees decrease, again cet. par.

f. a shift of the payment system from fee-for-service to capitation;

A shift of the payment system from fee-for-service to capitation may decrease health care expenditures and decrease payments to providers, thus increasing the insurer's profit.

10.3   Explain the differences among the following three types of government intervention in the health insurance market: (1) public subsidy, (2) mandated insurance benefits, and (3) direct public provision of insurance coverage. If the goal of government intervention is to achieve universal coverage, which strategy is the best (most efficient) in terms of minimizing the deadweight loss?

The public subsidy reduces the relative price of health insurance and hence provides an incentive for individuals to purchase private health insurance. A public subsidy can be implemented as a fixed dollar income transfer from the government to the individual, irrespective of the amount of insurance the individual purchases. This type of subsidy per se may not alter the price of insurance relative to other goods. But the subsidy is typically only available for the purchase of a qualified health insurance plan. Thus, the subsidy would increase the demand for private insurance coverage and create a deadweight loss. This increase in allocative inefficiency should be evaluated against the gain in equity that such a subsidy would provide.

Mandated insurance benefits require that an employer provide health insurance to its employees with a minimum set of benefits. Since this mandate increases the labor cost to the employer, it may adversely affect employment and wages. Thus, such a mandate is not an effective approach for achieving universal coverage.

Direct public provision occurs when the government provides public insurance program to all citizens or to the specific groups in the population. Public insurance may crowd out private health insurance if these two programs are available. Whether direct public provision is more efficient than a public subsidy for achieving the goal of universal coverage depends on many factors, including methods of financing, administrative cost, and flexibility of benefits to reflect heterogeneous preferences and circumstances of covered persons.

10.5   Compare differences between public health insurance and private health insurance on the following dimensions:

The following table summarizes differences between public health insurance and private health insurance:

	Public health insurance	Private health insurance
Diffusion of new medical technologies	Slow	Fast
Premium levels	Rigid	Flexible
Administrative expense	Low	High
Satisfying differences in consumer preferences	Low	High (at least sometimes)
Providing preventive services	High (sometimes)	Low (often)

a. the decision to adopt new medical technologies;

Public health insurers tend to adopt new medical technologies at a slower rate than private health insurers do. Private health insurers are in a better position to satisfy consumer preferences and to adjust premiums accordingly than public health insurers are. If consumers value new medical technologies, private health insurance are more likely to satisfy their preferences by offering coverage for new medical technologies. Since the adoption of the new medical technologies may be costly, private health insurers may charge a higher premium for such coverage. By contrast, public health insurer premiums tend to be rigid. That is, raising premiums often becomes a hot political issue. Given that increasing premiums is a difficult task, public health insurers tend to emphasize controlling costs over raising premiums as a result of offering a richer package of benefits. Since cost control often becomes a top priority of public health insurance programs, the decision to adopt new medical technologies tends to be slower.

b. premium setting;

Premiums are determined by market forces in the market for private health insurance. Insured persons pay more if they demand more comprehensive coverage. Thus, it is easy to raise premium and the only constraint for premium increases are market forces. By contrast, premium setting in the context of public insurance is determined by political forces. Also there are often many cross-subsidies across different groups of insured.

c. administrative expense;

Public health insurance is in a better position to save on administrative expense because of the larger size and lower cost of enrolling fewer persons. By contrast, private health insurers often need to market their products. There are often many competitors in markets for private health insurance.

d. satisfying differences in consumer preferences (consumer preference heterogeneity);

Since there are often many competitors in the market for private health insurance, consumers have many "choices" to satisfy their heterogeneous preferences. By contrast, with a public health insurance program, the government tends to offer a standard package to all citizens—a "one size fits all" package.

e. providing preventive services.

Since the public health insurance program often enjoys a monopoly position in the market, it can reap the entire future benefit of providing preventive services. Thus, public health insurance programs have a strong incentive to offer coverage of preventive services. By contrast, private health insurers often face many competitors in the market. They may not be in a position to capture the future benefit of providing preventive services to their insureds. Thus, incentives to offer preventive services are lower.

Chapter 11

Private Financing of Health Care Services

11.1   Use the concepts of cost of capital (COC) and marginal efficiency of investment (MEI) that you have learned in chapters 2 and 9 to analyze the effect of managed care on the diffusion of new and expensive medical technology in a hospital market. Present a graph to show how the growth of managed care affects COC and MEI for hospital investment in new technology. Justify your answer.

As we explained in chapter 10, managed care plans may pay less per unit of service for intensive treatments that use new medical technology and equipment, or they may delay coverage for new technology. This results in a decrease in expected profitability from adopting a new technology, which in turn reduces the marginal efficiency of investment (MEI) from adopting new technology. This shifts the MEI curve inward and hence reduces the level of the optimal engaging in R&D by medical device and diagnostic equipment companies and other firms involved in R&D. When prices paid to providers fall, their price-cost margins fall, which in turn, deters adoption of new technologies by hospitals and other types of health care providers.

11.3   Recall the discussion in chapter 5 about a long-run decision involving practice location. Suppose that the World Trade Organization (WTO) signed a treaty among all member countries guaranteeing no legal impediments to physician movement among countries. Physicians trained in one country could choose a practice location in any country in the world. Suppose you were a physician. Would the country's health care system be an important consideration in your choice of country in which to practice? If your choice were limited to cash versus private systems, which system would you prefer for your practice location, other things being equal? Explain the rationale for your choice.

The health care system affects how the price and quantities of health care services are determined which in turn affect physicians' income. Thus, the country's health care system is a very important factor in guiding a physician's choice of country in which to practice.

In a cash system, most revenues for physician services come from out-of-pocket payments. By contrast, in a private system, most revenue for physician services come from private health insurance. Given the evidence that the introduction of health insurance into a health care market leads to an increase in health expenditures, partly through the increase in the quantity of health care services demanded and through the increase in the price of health care, it is expected that physicians' income will increase under a private system relative to a cash system. Thus, other factors remaining equal, a private system is more attractive to physicians than a cash system is.

According to what we have learned in chapter 4, a risk-adverse individual would choose to purchase health insurance to avoid the expenditure risk arising from the uncertainty of becoming ill. In addition, an individual may pay more for maintaining good health as the individual's income rises. International comparisons of health expenditures show a strong positive relationship between national income and health expenditures. This suggests that the share of out-of-pocket (OOP) payments as a share of total health expenditures declines as income rises because the demand for health insurance increases as people become more affluent. There should be a negative relationship between the share of OOP payments and the income level if there is no government regulation to restrict the entry of insurers.

Chapter 12

Government Financing and Private Supply

12.1   Define "retrospective cost-based reimbursement system" and "prospective payment system." Suppose you were asked by a policy maker to design the payment system for a public insurance program. If the policy maker would like to use the payment system to achieve the goal of cost containment, which payment system you would recommend? If the policy maker changes the goal of policy and would like to focus on increasing the quality of health care, would you change your recommendation for the design of the payment system? Justify your recommendation.

A retrospective cost-based reimbursement system is a payment system in which the amount of payment to hospitals for providing health care services is based on actual costs incurred when they are provided. A prospective payment system is a payment system in which the amount of payment to hospitals for providing health care services is specified in advance.

Under retrospective cost reimbursement, hospitals have little or no incentive to cut cost because hospitals generate more revenue by raising cost. By contrast, under prospective payment, hospitals have a strong incentive to reduce cost because the payment level is fixed in advance and hence hospitals gain by reducing cost. Thus, a prospective payment system is better for achieving the goal of cost containment.

Our recommendation on the design of payment system may change if the policy objective is to increase the quality of health care. This is because hospitals do not have a direct financial incentive to increase quality of health care under a prospective payment system. In some specific situations, the effort of reducing cost under prospective payment system may harm quality, e.g., if patients are discharged quickly but sicker. Note that there is no direct evidence that this occurred when US Medicare switched from a retrospective to a prospective method of paying hospitals. A pay-for-performance system may offer greater promise in achieving the goal of increasing quality. A pay-for-performance system makes payment a function of achieving specific quality goals, as measured by pre-specified quality of care indicators.

12.3   Suppose country A traditionally relies on out-of-pocket costs to finance personal health care services. Assume this country receives a substantial amount of foreign aid for its many infrastructure investments; hence the government can release public funds to finance personal health care services. Suppose the government decides to introduce an additional system of universal coverage through a single-payer program. Conceptually, what effect do you expect the introduction of universal coverage to have on the demand and supply sides of the country's health care market? List at least two impacts on both sides of the health care market in country A. Justify each effect you list.

On the demand side, the introduction of universal coverage is likely to have two effects. First, demand for health care will increase as the implementation of universal coverage reduces patients' out-of-pocket cost. That is, health care utilization will increase. Second, as the burden of out-of-pocket payments decreases, the demand for higher quality health care services may increase.

On the supply side, the introduction of universal coverage increases market demand for health care. This implies that the size of the hospital market increases and hence the revenue from hospital services increases, too. As a result, implementation of universal coverage will induce more hospitals to enter the market. In addition, as demand for quality increases, hospitals may have an added incentive to increase investment in new medical technologies.

12.5 Finkelstein (2007) reported that implementation of the Medicare program in the United States led to a 37 percent increase in real hospital expenditures between 1965 and 1970. However, based on estimates from the Rand HIE study (see chapter 3), the implementation of Medicare increased real hospital expenditures by only 5.6 percent. Explain the differences between these two estimates.

The estimates from the RAND HIE are based on a partial equilibrium analysis which assumes that the supply side of health care market does not change when insurance coverage expands. By contrast, Finkelstein's analysis (2007) is based on a general equilibrium framework that considers changes in both demand and supply sides of the market. Introducing health insurance reduces out-of-pocket payments which in turn increases demand for health care services. As market demand increases, the supply side of health care is likely to respond in several ways, including entry of new hospitals, R&D investments to develop new technologies, and adoption of such new medical technologies. These supply-side responses in turn lead to a further increase in health care costs. Therefore, we observe a larger increase in health expenditures under a general-equilibrium analysis than in a partial-equilibrium analysis.

12.7 Use three graphs to show the effect of Medicaid fees on the physician's incentive to accept Medicaid patients. Graph A is a horizontal line that represents the demand curve for Medicaid patients. Graph B is a downward-sloping curve that represents the demand curve for non-Medicaid patients. Graph C represents the sum of demand from the two separate markets. Assume that the physician's marginal cost curve has a positive slope. Show:

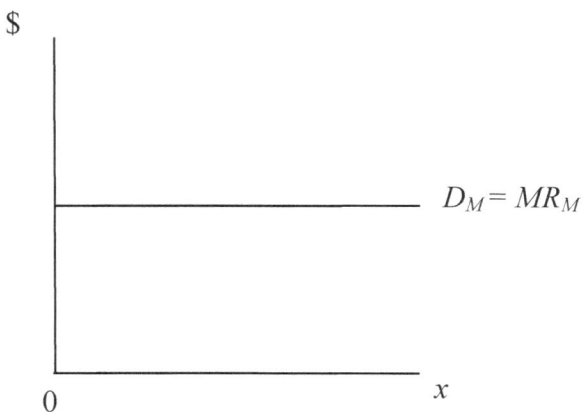

Graph A: Medicaid patients' demand curve

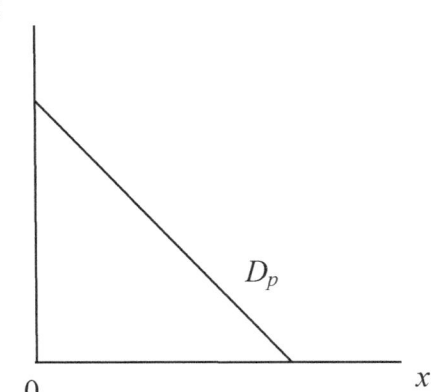

Graph B: Private (Non-Medicaid) patients' demand curve

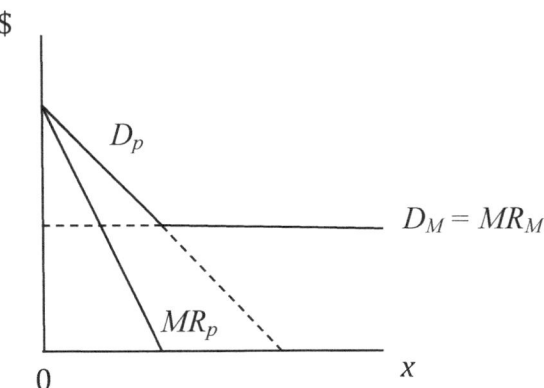

Graph C: Sum of demand from the above two markets

a. How will the physician set the price for non-Medicaid patients if the physician pursues maximum profit?

The physician sets the price for non-Medicaid patients by equating marginal revenue (MR) and marginal cost (MC). At the intersection point of MC and MR, the physician determines the optimal quantity of health services (x^*). Then, the physician sets the price at p^* along the demand curve.

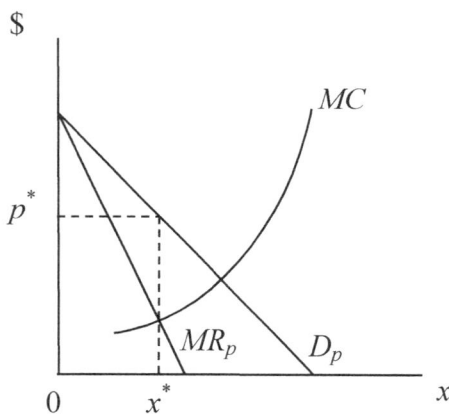

b. Under what conditions will the physician not accept Medicaid patients? Show graphically.

The physician will not accept Medicaid patients if the fee schedule set by the payer is set at or below p_M, that is at or below the intersection point of MC and MR_p, as shown in the following figure.

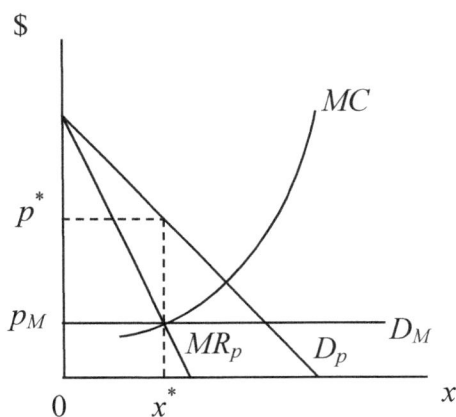

c. Will the physician be more likely to accept Medicaid patients if the government increases the Medicaid fees paid to the physician? Show the effect of an increased Medicaid fee graphically.

For Medicaid price p_m, the marginal revenue curve declines from p_0 to A and, for additional output, coincides with p_m. Equilibrium is at the point A' where $MC = MR$.

After the Medicaid price rises from p_m to p_m', the new MR curve goes from p_0 to B and then along p_m'. The new intersection of MC and MR is at B'. Total output rises. However, output to the private market declines, the physician becomes a participant in the Medicaid program and supplies an amount of output to Medicaid recipients equal to the length of segment BB'.

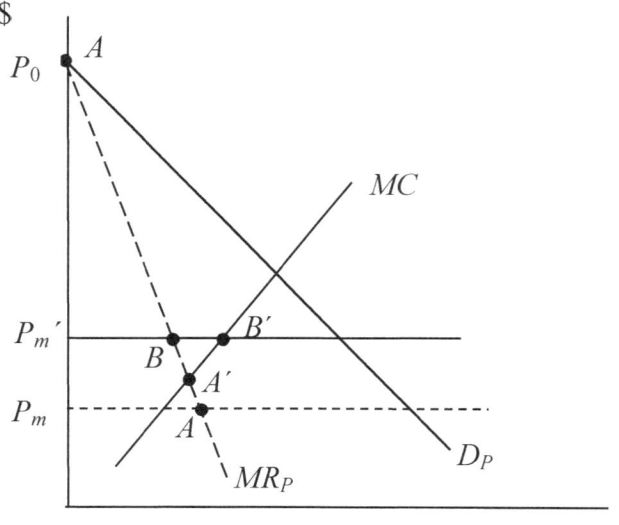

12.9   Assume a country's health care expenditures (HCE) are financed from two sources: (1) public expenditures (PE) and (2) out-of-pocket payments (OOP). Thus, HCE = PE + OOP. Given the following relationships: (PE/HCE) + (OOP/HCE) = 1 and HCE/GDP = PE/GDP + OOP/GDP, where GDP represents the gross domestic product. Suppose this country currently spends 5 percent of GDP on personal health care and services, and out-of-pocket payments account for 60 percent of the country's total health care expenditures. Use the above-mentioned information and relationships to answer the following questions:

a. If the government increases funding for personal health care services by adding 1 percent of GDP to health care, and assuming that other things remain constant, that is, the share of GDP spent on health care (HCE/GDP) remains unchanged, will this policy reduce the share of out-of-pocket payments on health care expenditure (OOP/HCE)? Calculate the new values of OOP/HCE under this scenario.

PE/GDP = (PE/HCE)(HCE/GDP). Since PE/HCE = 0.4 and HCE/GDP = 0.05, PE/GDP = 0.02.
Similarly, OOP/GDP = (OOP/HCE)(HCE/GDP). Since OOP/HCE = 0.6 and HCE/GDP = 0.05, OOP/GDP = 0.03.

This suggests that PE/GDP increases from 0.02 to 0.03 but HCE/GDP remain constant (at 0.05). This implies that OOP/GDP = 0.02 because OOP/GDP = (HCE/GDP)-(PE/GDP). We then calculate OOP/HCE = (OOP/GDP)/(HCE/GDP) = 0.02/0.05 = 0.4.

Now out-of-pocket payments account for 40% of total health care expenditures.

b. If the new funds injected into the health care sector lead providers to raise fees, with the result that HCE/GDP increases from 5 percent to 6 percent, will this policy reduce the share of out-of-pocket payments in the health care expenditure? Calculate the new value of OOP/HCE under this scenario.

Given the condition that PE/GDP = 0.03 and HCE/GDP = 0.06, OOP/GDP = 0.03 and OOP/HCE = 0.5 according to the above two formulas. That is, out-of-pocket payments now account for 50% of total health care expenditures.

c. If the new funds injected into a health care system induce a high rate of health care inflation caused by increased wasteful health care spending, with the result that HCE/GDP increases from 5 percent to 10 percent, will this policy reduce the share of out-of-pocket payments in total health care expenditures? Calculate the new value of OOP/HCE under this scenario.

Given the condition that PE/GDP = 0.03 and HCE/GDP = 0.10, OOP/GDP = 0.07 and OOP/HCE = 0.7 according to the above two formulas. That is, out-of-pocket payments now account for 70% of total health care expenditures.

d. Based on the scenarios in parts (a) to (c) of this question, explain how a government could use the new funds to promote effective and efficient health care provision so that the new public sector funds lead to a reduction in the share of out-of-pocket payments in total health care expenditures. Under what conditions would the government fail to achieve this policy goal, with the new funds being captured by providers in the form of higher income and profits?

If injection of new public funds into the public sector does not lead to an increase in health care expenditures, i.e., the HCE/GDP ratio remains constant, then the public funds will substitute for private funds to finance health care. In this case, the policy of increasing public funds will lead to a decrease in the share of out-of-pocket payments in total health expenditures. If injection of new public funds into the public sector leads to an increase in health care expenditures, that is, the HCE/GDP ratio increases, then an increase in public funds may not be necessary to reduce the share of out-of-pocket payments in total health care expenditures. If the magnitude of the health expenditure increase is larger than the magnitude of new public funds, then the share of out-of-pocket payments in total health expenditures will increase.

Chapter 13

Public Supply and Financing

13.1   For which of the following services is public supply likely to be superior to private supply? Discuss each service and justify your answers.

Public supply is most likely to be superior to private supply	Private supply is most likely to be superior to public supply
Prisons Schooling (compulsory education) Vaccinations	Housing

a. prison;

If the private sector provides prison services, the firm may have a strong incentive to cut cost than to improve quality. Due to the noncontractible nature of prison services, the adverse effect of cost reduction on noncontractible quality is sufficiently large. Thus, public provision of prison service seems better than private supply to avoid the adverse effect of cost reductions.

b. schooling;

With regard to schooling, if the policy goal is to achieve the universal education, then public provision may be better than private supply because private schools may have strong incentive to cut cost, adversely affecting the goal of "compulsory schooling." However, if schooling involves noncompulsory education, such as higher education, then neither public nor private provision can be said to be generally preferred. This depends on whether or not the government can prevent quality deterioration arising from various types of cost cutting.

c. vaccination;

As mentioned in the text, vaccinations generate important external benefits to society. Since individuals would not take such external benefits into account in making their decisions on whether or not to be vaccinated, there is a tendency toward undersupply if vaccinations are private. Thus public provision for vaccination may be superior to private supply.

d. housing.

Housing provides an example when private supply is most likely to be superior to public supply because consumers are able to monitor both cost reductions and quality improvements in housing supply. Thus, private supply is more likely to be efficient than is public supply in satisfying consumer preferences.

13.3   Collect data on GDP per capita and percentage of out-of-pocket payment in total health expenditures for at least twenty countries from any data set you can access (e.g., OECD Health Data or the World Health Statistics 2016 [WHO 2016]). Plot the data, with GDP per capita on the horizontal axis and percentage of out-of-pocket payment on the vertical axis, and answer the following questions:

a. Based on your figure, is there any clear relationship between GDP per capita and percentage of out-of-pocket payment? If so, does the relationship have a negative or a positive slope? How do you interpret such a relationship?

Requires student figure.

b. Did any country become an outlier in your figure? How do you explain this exception?

Requires student figure.

13.5   In recent years, government revenues from taxing tobacco and selling lottery tickets have been widely used to finance health care provision and services. Suppose both China and India were to adopt a major health care reform to reduce their citizens' share of out-of-pocket payment in total health expenditure, but each country decides to use a different funding source. China uses a tobacco tax and the net revenue from selling lottery tickets as the source of public funds; India uses the personal income tax as its source of public funds. Assume that other aspects remain constant. Compare the equity in health care financing between these two countries.

If we accept the criteria of "ability to pay" to define "equity" in health care financing, then we can measure vertical equity by examining whether or not individuals or families with high incomes (high ability to pay) contribute more to health care financing than their counterparts with low incomes. It has been widely recognized in the literature that personal income taxes are more progressive than are indirect taxes such as an excise tax on tobacco products. If India uses the personal income tax as its source of public funds, we would expect that more affluent persons would pay a larger proportion of their incomes on personal health care services than the poor. By contrast, the poor tend to be more likely to buy lottery tickets than the rich. In addition, tobacco taxes are a form of indirect that impose a selectively higher burden on the poor.

Thus, we can expect that low-income individuals would pay a higher proportion of their incomes on personal health care services than the rich if China were to use a tobacco tax and net revenue from selling lottery tickets as the source of public funds. Therefore, we expect that India would be in a better position than China in achieving the goal of vertical equity in health care financing.

13.7   Many countries have a "mixed" health care system, that is, a private health care sector exists alongside a larger public health care sector. Under such a system, individuals may choose to "opt out" of the public system and receive care from private sources. Does this opting-out behavior occur more frequently in low-income countries than in high-income countries? Why or why not? Do the major drivers that induce people to opt out the public system differ between high-income and low-income countries?

Without appealing to empirical evidence, it is hard to reach a general conclusion about whether or not opting out behavior occurs more frequently in low-income countries than in high-income countries. This is because the relative quality of health care services between public and private sectors might vary substantially among countries. However, it has been widely recognized that the driving force that induces people to opt out of the public system differs between low-income and high-income countries. In low-income countries, the quality of health care services provided in the public sector tends to be lower than in the private sector. Thus, seeking for high-quality care is the major reason for opting out of public care in low-income countries. By contrast, in high-income countries, the quality difference between the public and private sector tends not to be a big issue. Rather, people opt out the public system to avoid a long waiting time in terms of time to an appointment, waiting time in the physician's office or clinic or both.

Chapter 14

Cost and Cost-Effectiveness Analysis

14.1 **Given the information listed in table 14.1, suppose that 1,000 individuals are in the poor health state in period t and θ_{PG} is 0.45, θ_{PP} is 0.40, and θ_{PD} is 0.15 without the drug. With the drug, the probabilities are 0.65, 0.30, and 0.05, respectively. Compute the number of persons in each health state over three years if people do not take the drug. Similarly, compute the number of persons in each health state over three years if people do take the drug.**

Number of persons in each health state if people do not take the drug

Health Status	Year 1	Year 2	Year 3
Good health	450 (1000×0.45)	400×0.45 $+ 450 \times 1 = 630$	$160 \times 0.45 + 630 \times 1 = 702$
Poor Health	400 (1000×0.40)	$400 \times 0.40 = 160$	$160 \times 0.40 = 64$
Death	150 (1000×0.15)	$400 \times 0.15 = 60$	$160 \times 0.15 = 24$
Total	1,000	850	790

Note: Assume $\theta_{GG} = 1$.

Number of persons in each health state if people take the drug

Health Status	Year 1	Year 2	Year 3
Good health	650	195 + 650 = 845	845 + 59 = 904
Poor health	300	90	27
Death	50	15	4
Total	1,000	950	935

Note: Assume $\theta_{GG} = 1$.

14.3   Referring to chapter 2, suppose you were asked the following trade-off question. Assume you had a particular disease (you need to pick a specific disease) and there was a surgical operation that would (1) either cure you of the disease completely, and you would be in perfect health, *or* (2) possibly kill you during the operation, painlessly and quickly. Would you choose to have the operation if the chance of dying was 15 percent?

According to equation (2.6),

$$U_b = (1 - \theta^*)U_a + \theta^* U_d \tag{2.6}$$

where U_a is the person's utility when perfectly healthy, U_d is utility when dead, U_b is the person's utility with the disease, θ^* is the probability of dying painlessly and quickly during the operation that makes the person indifferent between undergoing the operation or not. Set U_a to 1.0 and U_d to 0.0, then we obtain $U_b = 0.85$ if $\theta^* = 0.15$.

Recall that the U_b can be interpreted as a measure of QALYs. Therefore, we can conclude that the individual will not choose to have the operation if his or her current QALY is greater than 0.85.

Chapter 15

Measuring Benefits and Cost-Benefit Analysis

15.1   Lichtenberg (2001) estimated the benefits and costs of newer drugs. The results are summarized as follow:

Mean Effect of Switching from 15 Year-Old Drugs to 5.5-Year-Old Drugs on Expenditures for Entire Population (in US$)

Expenditure Type	Mean Effect
Prescription drugs	18
Hospital	−80
Home health care	−12
Office visits	−24
Outpatient	−10
Emergency room	−3

Note: Negative signs indicate reductions in spending.

a. Based on the above findings, identify the benefits of using newer drugs.

The benefits of using newer drugs include the savings in hospital expenditures, the savings in spending on home health care, office visits, outpatient services and emergency room visits.

b. Given the above information, do you have enough information to conduct a CBA for using newer drugs? Justify your answer.

The information given is not sufficient to allow cost-benefit analysis of newer drugs to be conducted. This is because the information given only includes the benefits arising from the savings in health expenditures from other components of health care services. The benefits of using new drugs may also include a reduction in mortality, an increase in the quality of life as well as an increase in labor productivity. However, the information on these benefits is not available for the exercise.

15.3   Bishai and Lang (2000) used the stated preference approach to estimate the WTP for a one-month reduction in a waiting time for cataract surgery. They found that an average cataract patient in Barcelona, Spain, would be willing to pay US$107 (in 1992 prices) for a reduction in waiting time of one month. But the same WTP estimate for an average cataract patient in Denmark is only US$24. Their study also reports that 40 percent of cataract surgeries in Barcelona are performed in the private sector to avoid the waiting time in the public sector. By contrast, only 15 percent of cataract surgeries in Denmark are performed in the private sector. How would you use the information on the ratio of cataract surgeries performed in the private sector across countries to judge the validity of this study?

The maximum willingness to pay (WTP) for a reduction in waiting time represents the demand for opting out of the public system. That is, individuals are more likely to opt out of the public system and use the services provided by the private sector if their WTP for a reduction in waiting time is higher. In this case, the positive relationship between the estimates of WTP and the percentage of patients who choose to opt out the public system is consistent with the theoretical prediction. Thus, the study is valid.

Chapter 16

The Contribution of Personal Health Services to Longevity, Population Health, and Economic Growth

16.1 Collect data on health expenditures per capita (HE) and life expectancy at birth (LE) for at least fifteen countries in a given year, and run a simple regression in which LE is the dependent variable and HE is the independent variable. You can obtain data for these two variables from the World Development Indicators published by the World Bank. What is the sign of your estimated coefficient? Is the parameter estimate statistically significant at the 5 percent level? How do you interpret your result? What kind of "bias" might you have from this simple regression?

Country name	Country code	Health expenditure per capita (current US$)	Life expectancy at birth (years)
Australia	AUS	3867.43	81.54
Austria	AUT	5037.31	80.08
Belgium	BEL	5104.02	80.63
Canada	CAN	4379.76	81.22
Czech Rep.	CZE	1383.65	77.08
Denmark	DNK	6272.73	78.60
Estonia	EST	1004.43	74.82
Finland	FIN	4309.60	79.72
France	FRA	4797.97	81.07
Germany	DEU	4628.77	79.94
Greece	GRC	3040.73	80.19
Hungary	HUN	937.99	73.90
Iceland	ISL	3130.39	81.46

Ireland	IRL	4951.84	79.50
Israel	ISR	1966.47	81.55
Italy	ITA	3327.63	81.44
Japan	JPN	3321.47	82.93
Korea, Rep.	KOR	1107.95	80.28
Luxembourg	LUX	8182.86	80.09
Netherlands	NLD	5163.74	80.55
New Zealand	NZL	2633.62	80.30
Norway	NOR	7661.61	80.80
Poland	POL	803.65	75.70
Portugal	PRT	2409.66	78.73
Slovak Rep.	SVK	1372.69	74.91
Slovenia	SVN	2174.72	78.97
Spain	ESP	3075.01	81.53
Sweden	SWE	4251.98	81.35
Switzerland	CHE	7140.73	82.04
United Kingdom	GBR	3285.05	80.05
United States	USA	7410.16	78.66

Source: World Development Indicators 2009.

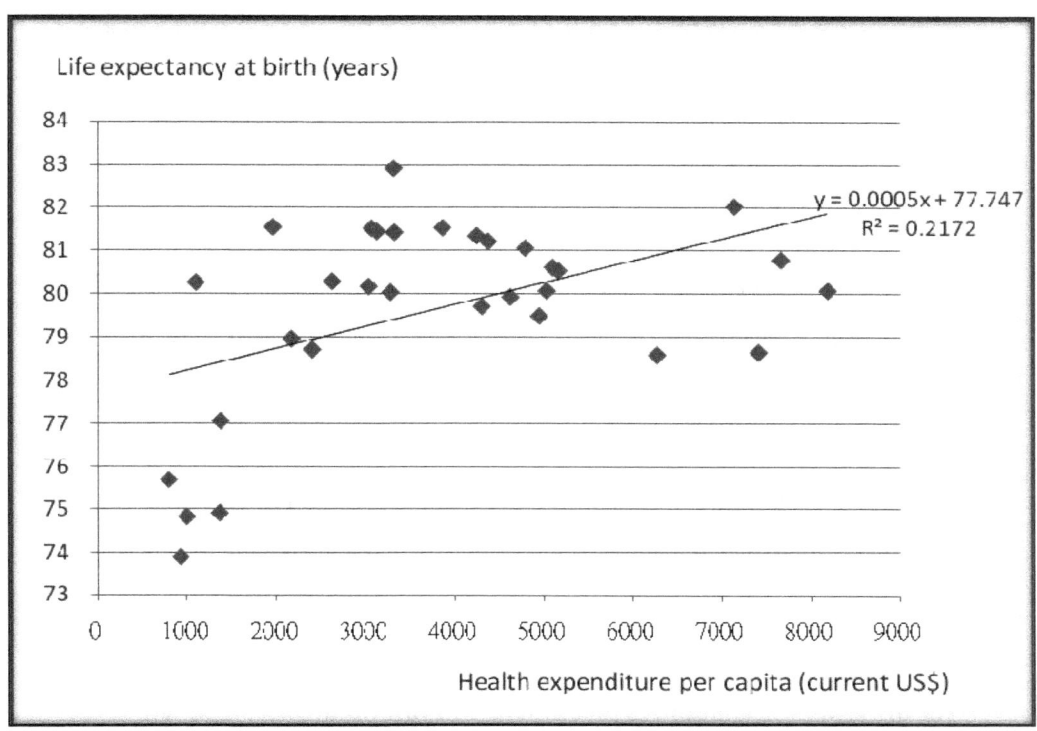

The parameter estimate is positive and statistically significant at the one percent level. This suggests that a higher health expenditure per capita leads to a higher life expectancy at birth. Since population health is also influenced by many other factors, such as choices in lifestyle, the simple regression may be subject to "omitted variable bias," in this case an upward bias in estimating the effect of medical care input on health output.

16.3 **Use the concept of marginal efficiency of investment (MEI) and cost of capital (COC) described in chapters 2 and 9, and extend this framework to consider how parents decide the optimal year of educational investment for their children. Draw the MEI and COC lines on a graph, with the amount of educational investment (which could be measured by the number of years in school) on the *x*-axis and the rate on the *y*-axis. What are the shapes of the MEI and COC schedules? Explain intuitively why they look as they do. Based on this framework, can you predict the effect of reduction in mortality on the parents' optimal investment in education for their children? Justify your answer.**

As in figures 2.1 and 9.1, the COC is a horizontal line. The MEI curve has a negative slope, indicating that the rate of return from schooling declines as the years of schooling increases. The reduction in child mortality implies that the expected returns from formal education increases because work lives have been extended. This is associated with an outward shift of the MEI curve. Hence, we can expect that parents will increase their optimal investment in children's education as child mortality declines.